Flynt • Cooter

Comprehensive Reading Inventory,

Third Edition

(CRI–3)

STUDENT BOOKLET (SB)

E. Sutton Flynt

Kathleen Spencer Cooter
Bellarmine University

Robert B. Cooter, Jr.
Bellarmine University

 Pearson

Library of Congress Cataloging-in-Publication Data

Cataloging-in-Publication Data is available on file at the Library of Congress

2 2021

ISBN 10:   0-13-524259-2
ISBN 13: 978-01-35-24259-9

CONTENTS

> **IMPORTANT:** This product is sold as a two-book set (ISBN: 9780135210048) that includes an **EXAMINER'S MANUAL** (ISBN: 9780135243626) and this **STUDENT BOOKLET** (ISBN: 9780135242599). You will need both books to administer and score the CRI-3.

FORM D   EXPOSITORY PASSAGES: Fall Term

FORM E   Expository Passages: Winter Term

FORM F   EXPOSITORY PASSAGES: Spring Term

FORM G   EXPOSITORY PASSAGES FOR GRADES 10-12: Fall Term

EARLY/EMERGENT LITERACY ASSESSMENTS (PRE K – 1)

Letter Naming Test (LNT)

Student Form 1:
Alphabet Letter Display (Mixed-Case Letters)

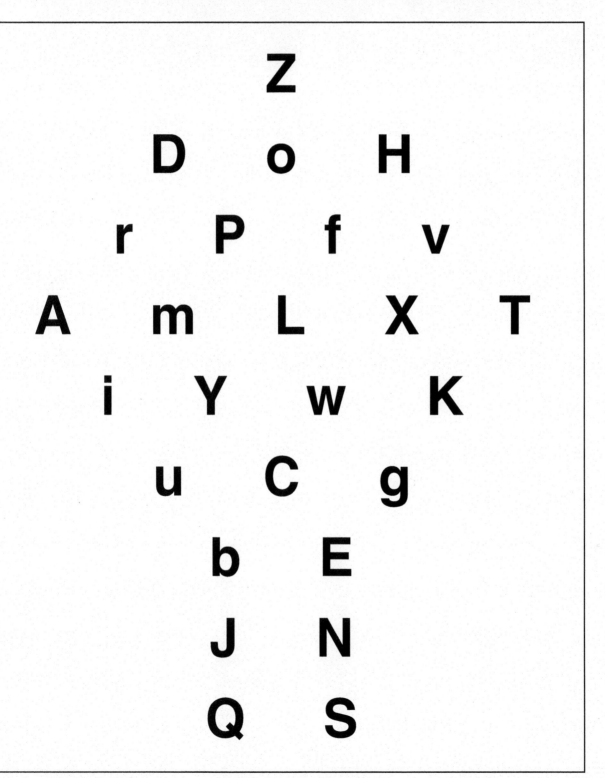

Letter Naming Test (LNT)

Student Form 2:
Alphabet Letter Display (All Uppercase Letters)

Z

D O H

R P F V

A M L X T

I Y W K

U C G

B E

J N

Q S

Letter Naming Test (LNT)

Student Form 3:
Alphabet Letter Display (All Lowercase Letters)

z

d   o   h

r   p   f   v

a   m   l   x   t

i   y   w   k

u   c   g

b   e

j   n

q   s

Phonics Test (PT)
Student Form

1.	dunk	zip	born
2.	fight	claw	pining
3.	sunk	quench	batting
4.	bashed	soup	lads
5.	viper	yapping	cod
6.	fur	note	leg
7.	holly	winter	boat
8.	taper	police	labor

Phonics Test (PT)
Student Form (Continued)

9.	car	veal	relay
10.	nice	sub	wisp
11.	drop	font	butter
12.	babble	sheet	leek
13.	home	catnip	shade
14.	fade	jogging	chapel
15.	windy	fishes	waist
16.	chain	number	discover

High-Frequency Word Knowledge Survey (HFWKS)
Student Record Form

Student's Name _____

Date Tested _____

> **Directions:** *Circle any words the student does* not *know.*

the	of	and	a	to	in
is	you	that	it	he	was
for	on	are	as	with	his
they	I	at	be	this	have
from	or	one	had	by	words
but	not	what	all	were	we
when	your	can	said	there	use
an	each	which	she	do	how
their	if	will	up	other	about
out	many	then	them	these	so
some	her	would	make	like	him
into	time	has	look	two	more
write	go	see	number	no	way
could	people	my	than	first	water
been	called	who	oil	its	now
find	long	down	day	did	get
come	made	may	part		

SENTENCES FOR INITIAL PASSAGE SELECTION - FALL TERM (F)

FORM A

He wanted to fly.

The family got together.

The boy was jumping.

Jim quickly walked to town to see a friend.

She was unhappy about leaving the party last Saturday.

I was pulled out of the lake.

It was fall and the forest was changing colors.

I was sleeping when my mother called with the news.

Summer vacation would begin on May 29 next school year.

I like being the youngest in our family.

My grandmother insisted on watching the television show daily.

Trivia games are sometimes boring to me, but I do learn new facts every time.

Shoes come in all styles and colors.

Serious athletes always practice a lot to become the best at their sport.

A cheap pair of running shoes doesn't last very long because of the pounding they take on roadways.

Mark was searching for evidence that someone had climbed the mountain before his arrival.

Maria realized the rock formation was too high for hiking on her short holiday.

The state conservationist hoped to reforest the valley to prevent further erosion.

Unfortunately, Kim was confused about the next activity to be completed in geology class.

Submerged rocks were hazardous to swimmers and caused officials to cancel the event.

Adam disappeared around the bend in the river at an alarming rate of speed that left rescuers behind.

Ascending the mountain was both rigorous and menacing for the expedition team.

The famous cliff provided a panoramic view of the Grand Canyon in spite of the weather conditions.

The incubation period for chickenpox is from ten to twenty-one days and a person is contagious for about a week.

Abduction of the young superstar shocked the community and led to calls for new legislation.

Detective Smith was inundated with questions regarding the special inquiry into the disappearance.

Sara's physical evaluation was extended because her complexion made her appear older than her chronological age.

NARRATIVE READING PASSAGES: FALL TERM

I Can Fly!

Sam wanted to fly.

His family said, "You cannot fly."

Sam jumped from a box.

He jumped from his bed.

Sam could not fly.

One day a letter came for Sam.

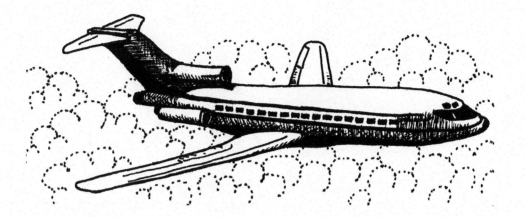

It was from his grandfather.

The letter said, "Come and see me on the airplane."

Sam's parents read the letter.

Sam said, "Now I can fly!"

Sam and his family laughed.

The Pig and Snake

One day Mr. Pig was walking to town for groceries.

Along the way he saw a hole beside the road and became curious.

There was a huge snake in the hole. Mr. Pig said to the snake, "Who put you in that hole?"

The snake said, "Help me and I will always be your friend. You can trust me."

"No!" said Mr. Pig. "If I help you get out of the hole you will bite me. You are a snake and that is what snakes do!"

The snake started to cry.

Feeling sorry for the snake, Mr. Pig decided to pull the snake from the hole. "There," said Mr. Pig, "now you can live a happy life."

A few minutes later the snake said, "Now that I feel better, I think I will bite you."

"Wait! How can you bite me after I helped you out of the hole?" said Mr. Pig.

The snake smiled and said, "You knew I was a snake when you pulled me from the hole!"

Zeke's New Dog

This is a special day for Zeke. It is his birthday and his parents said he could have his first dog. "Having a dog is a big job," said Zeke's dad, "they can live for as much as 15 years. So, I think we should learn how to choose and care for a dog."

Mom, Dad, Zeke, and his baby sister went to see a veterinarian near their home. They wanted advice on how to choose a dog. Dr. Brigett Sands, the veterinarian, said, "The first thing to think about is the dog's breed since that will tell you how much exercise he will need. Some dogs need lots of exercise, others need less. Golden Retrievers and Beagles need lots of exercise. Bulldogs and many little dogs do not need as much exercise."

After leaving the veterinarian's office they talked more about the kind of dog they would adopt. "Dr. Sands said that puppies are not always good around young children," said Dad. "We should try to adopt a smaller dog a few months old. It will still be a puppy but good around the baby. A little dog would make sense, too, since we live in an apartment."

"May our new dog sleep in my room?" asked Zeke. "Probably. The vet said that dogs need a warm and quiet place to rest. So, I think she would say that the puppy could sleep in your room" said Dad. "She also said we need to get a training crate. That is a kind of cage for dogs with room for a bed. Dogs like sleeping in a crate and feel safe. Your job will be to take the dog outside when she first wakes up in the morning. That will help her learn where to go to the bathroom."

Zeke and his family went to an animal shelter near their home. There were so many wonderful dogs to adopt. The entire family fell in love with a young dog that was a "mix" breed. This is a dog that is a mixture of two or more different breeds such as a Poodle and Golden Retriever mix. Mix-breeds are wonderful dogs and can be very smart. They chose a five-month-old girl puppy. She was a small, furry dog with a long body, short stubby legs, and blond in color. Zeke named her Kate and she went home with her new family that very same day, wagging her tail the whole time.

New Clothes

Bobby was the youngest member of his family. He really didn't like being the youngest of three kids. For one thing, he wasn't allowed to stay up late. Most of all, he disliked having to wear his big brother's hand-me-down clothes.

One day Bobby was upset and went to his mother and said, "Mom, I'm tired of wearing Brad's old clothes all the time. Why can't I have some new clothes of my own?"

His mother replied, "Bobby, you know we do not have enough money to buy new clothes. Try to be happy with the clothes we are able to offer you. Besides, Brad hardly ever wore those nice clothes."

As Bobby walked away, his mother said, "Bobby, if you can find a way to earn some money, I'll see what I can do to help."

Bobby thought and thought. Finally, he had a brilliant idea. Brad and his sister, Sara, had part-time jobs and they didn't always have time to do their chores. What if he did some of their work for money?

Bobby approached Brad and Sara about his new idea. They liked his plan and agreed to pay Bobby money for cleaning their rooms and making their beds.

As Bobby turned to leave the room, Sara said, "Bobby, remember to do a thorough job or we will have to pay you less."

Bobby took care of their rooms for four weeks and did a great job. Finally, on the last Saturday before school started, Bobby's mom took him shopping at the mall. Bobby got to pick out a pair of popular jeans and a new shirt. On the first day of school, Bobby felt proud of his new clothes that he had worked so hard to buy. His mother was even more proud.

Great Shoes

All the boys at Anthony Middle School loved the new athletic shoes. Some wore the "Sky High" model by Leader. Some liked the "Street Smarts" by Master, or the "Uptown-Downtown" by Beebop. The boys were even able to identify their friends just by looking at their feet! But the boy who was the envy of the school was Jamie Lee. He had a pair of "High Five Pump'em Ups" by Superior. The only thing the boys loved more than their shoes was basketball. They would lace up their fancy shoes and play basketball all afternoon. Everyone was convinced that their high-priced shoes helped them jump higher and run faster.

One day a new student appeared on the playground named Josh Kidder. He wore a cheap pair of black high-top basketball shoes made by an old-fashioned company called White Dot. When Jamie Lee saw Josh's White Dot shoes, he said, "No serious basketball player wears White Dots anymore. Where have you been, Kidder?"

Josh said, "Well, I may not have an expensive pair of shoes like yours, but I'd still like to play basketball with you and the other guys." Jamie Lee and the other boys kind of chuckled and said, "Sure kid, not a problem."

What happened next is now a matter of history at Anthony Middle School. Josh ran faster, jumped higher, and scored more points than anybody else that day. Jamie Lee, who was guarded by Josh, managed only two points. When it was all over the boys gathered around Josh. He was the hero of the day and everyone asked, "What's your secret?"

Josh just smiled widely and said, "Two things—lots of practice and cheap shoes." Everyone laughed.

Mountain Fire

One August afternoon Brad and Kevin went tracking with Brad's father on Mount Holyoak. Brad's father was a conservationist for the Forest Service and was searching for evidence of cougars. Many people feared that the cougars were becoming extinct on Mount Holyoak and wanted to take steps to save the species. The boys became excited when they found what appeared to be cougar tracks near a stream. But as the day wore on no new tracks were found.

After lunch Brad's father sent the boys upstream while he circled west searching for more cougar tracks. He told the boys to return to the lunch site in an hour whether they found tracks or not. After about forty-five minutes the boys found the stream's source and could follow it no more. So, they decided to search close to the stream for evidence of cougars before starting back. They photographed rock formations, eagles' nests on high ledges and, finally, two fresh cougar footprints. Both boys were very excited until they realized that they no longer could hear the stream. In short, they were lost.

The boys searched an hour or more for the mountain stream or a cell phone signal, but without success. They were tired, dirty, and getting worried. Brad decided to start a small fire in hopes of his father seeing the smoke. Kevin reminded Brad of the danger of forest fires but finally agreed to help collect the twigs, branches, and brush. The moment Brad struck a match in the extra-dry mountain air and stuck it to the dry tinder, the fire exploded into a large fireball.

In a matter of minutes, trees all around the boys burst into flames. The fire spread quickly up the mountainside. The boys ran downhill as fast as they could and called for help.

Before the day was over, firemen, airplanes carrying fire retardants, and bucket-loaded helicopters were on the scene trying to contain the fire. The fire raged for days, however, and more than 45,000 acres of timber had been consumed.

For several years Brad and Kevin spent every spare moment helping to reforest the mountain. One day a forest ranger commented, "Well, boys, it looks like things are about back to normal." Brad looked down and replied, "Maybe, but no new cougar tracks have been seen since the fire."

The Canoe Trip

Katherine and her family liked to spend their vacation camping out. Frequently they go to either Great Smoky Mountains National Park or Yellowstone National Park. Since they have camped out for many years, they have become quite accomplished. Katherine is able to start a fire with flint and steel, build a lean-to for shelter, and find food in the forest on which to live.

Katherine's favorite outdoor activity is canoeing. Although she is now an extremely competent canoer, there is one canoe trip that she'll never forget. It was a canoe trip she took with her family and her friend Amy down the beautiful Madison River near West Yellowstone, Montana.

Katherine and Amy were in a canoe together following her parents down the river at a gentle pace. The early going was fine, and they didn't have any major complications. The girls did get confused once or twice in their steering and the boat would go sideways. But after about thirty minutes on the river Katherine and Amy felt better about their ability to navigate the river. Unfortunately, their canoe could not keep up with Katherine's parents' canoe because they were carrying all the rations in two coolers. Slowly the lead canoe disappeared around a bend.

When the girls' canoe rounded the bend, not only could they not see the lead canoe, they were also heading directly into some rough white water. The rough water was swift and there were a lot of rocks submerged below the surface. The swiftness and rocks were causing problems for the jittery canoe and the two inexperienced girls. Fortunately, they were both wearing their helmets for safety.

Just as the canoe was about to clear the rough water, it struck a large boulder just beneath the surface. Before the girls knew what had happened, the canoe had capsized, sending them into the icy cold river. Naturally, they had on life jackets, so they were not in much danger. But the two coolers full of food and the canoe started floating away from them at a rapid rate.

Katherine managed to grab hold of the canoe and one paddle. Amy swam over to the shore. After a great deal of effort both girls managed to pull in the canoe, empty the water, and start downstream after the lost coolers. But since they had only one paddle they limped along, unable to catch up to their now disappeared coolers in the river's current.

Some forty-five minutes later, feeling cold and upset, the girls rounded a sharp bend in the river. To their surprise they saw the rest of the family sitting on the south-side shore of the river having a wonderful time. Katherine's dad had built a fire and was roasting hot dogs. Katherine's mother and little brother were sitting on the two coolers eating hot dogs and munching on potato chips. Dad said, "What took you two so long? We didn't know you were going to stop and take a swim, but thanks for sending the food on ahead." As cold as they were, Katherine and Amy couldn't help but laugh.

The Eagle

There is an ancient Native American legend about an eagle that thought he was a chicken. It seems that a Hopi farmer and his only son decided to ascend a nearby mountain to observe an eagle's nest. The trip would most assuredly take them all day, so they brought along rations and water for the long trek. The man and boy crossed the enormous fields of maize and beans that led to the foothills and soon thereafter they were scaling the mountain. The climb was both rigorous and hazardous, so they treated the mountain with great respect and took their time. Occasionally they looked back toward their home and took in the breathtaking panoramic view of the entire valley.

Finally, the farmer and son reached the mountain's summit and began searching for their prize. Eventually they discovered, perched on the highest point, a ledge with an eagle's nest. After realizing that the mother eagle had gone in search of food, the farmer cautiously reached his hand into the nest and brought out a most precious prize, an eagle's egg. He tucked it into his tunic to keep it safe and the two travelers began their slow descent to return to their village.

Once home, the farmer went to his coop and placed the egg in a chicken's nest for incubation, where it soon hatched. The eaglet grew up with the baby chicks and adopted their habits for gathering food in the barnyard—namely, scratching for feed the farmer threw out instead of searching for food the way eagles normally do.

Sometime later an Anasazi brave passed through the area and saw this enormous brown eagle scratching and walking about in the barnyard. He dismounted from his horse and went to the farmer and asked, "Why do you have an eagle acting like a chicken? This is not right," queried the noble brave.

"Why, that's no eagle, it's a chicken," retorted the farmer. "Can't you see that it scratches for food with the other chickens? No, it is indeed a chicken," exclaimed the farmer.

"I will show you that this is an eagle," said the brave.

The brave took the eagle on his arm and climbed to the top of the barn. Then saying, "You are an eagle, the most noble of birds. Fly and soar as you were destined!" he threw the eagle from the barn. But the startled eagle fluttered to the ground and began pecking for food.

"See," said the farmer. "I told you it is a chicken."

The brave replied, "I'll show you this is an eagle. It is clear what I must do."

Again the brave took the eagle on his arm and began walking toward the mountain. He climbed all day until he reached a high bluff overlooking the valley. Then the brave, with outstretched arm, held the bird out and said, "You are an eagle, the most noble of birds. Fly and soar as you were destined to do."

Just then a mountain breeze washed across the eagle. His eyes brightened as he caught the wild scent of freedom. In a moment, the eagle stretched his mighty wings and let out a magnificent screech. Leaping from the brave's arm, he flew high into the western sky.

The eagle saw more of the world in that one great moment than his barnyard friends would ever discover in a lifetime.

The Case of Miss Angela Violet

Angela Violet was an elderly lady in our neighborhood who some people thought seemed suspicious. She was rarely seen outside her spacious Victorian-styled home, and then only to retrieve her daily mail. Miss Violet's pasty complexion and ancient dress made her appear like an eerie apparition from a ghost story. Small children in the neighborhood speculated that she might be some sort of witch or sorceress. It certainly appeared that Miss Violet had absolutely no contact with the outside world.

One autumn day, news spread through the community that a high school cheerleader, Katrina Bowers, had disappeared on her way home from school. The police feared that Katrina had been abducted and issued an AMBER Alert. State and local police joined forces with the Federal Bureau of Investigation in the massive effort to find Katrina. In spite of all the best efforts of the constabulary, no trace of Katrina Bowers was discovered. After thirty days of fear, suspense, and worry, the police called off the search, but kept the case open. The police told her parents that in most cases like these the child would be found safe, but that did nothing to quell their fears.

Three weeks after Katrina's apparent abduction, a development in the case occurred. An anonymous telephone caller informed the police she thought Miss Angela Violet had kidnapped Katrina and was allegedly holding her captive in her basement. Because of Miss Violet's unusual lifestyle, the police were inclined to give some credence to the tip, so a search warrant was issued, and the police converged on her house.

Detective Donna Jordan knocked on the ancient door of Miss Violet's residence. Two other officers accompanied Detective Jordan. Miss Violet showed surprise but graciously welcomed the officers into her home. When asked, she even consented to having her home searched by the detectives. By the time the police had completed their search, two television news trucks had taken position outside her home. When the detectives came out of the house without Miss Violet, the anxious newspeople besieged them with queries.

Detective Jordan stepped forward and calmly said, "What we found was a kindly lady who is caring night and day for her ailing mother. There is no evidence whatsoever that Miss Violet has any involvement in the Katrina Bowers case."

Feeling embarrassed and obviously ashamed for judging her unfairly, people in the community began to reach out to Miss Violet and her mother from then on. They brought food and sat with Miss Violet's mother so she could get out of the house more often to shop and see friends. As for Katrina Bowers, she was located safe and sound in California with relatives. She had been a runaway and had never met Miss Violet.

SENTENCES FOR INITIAL PASSAGE SELECTION - WINTER TERM (W)

Today is my birthday party.

I wanted to have balloons and ice cream.

Mary stopped at the trees.

The storms made us have more maple leaves to rake this fall.

Marty needed some extra money to buy a present for Tom.

Jan heard me cooking breakfast in the kitchen.

Jeff was becoming afraid of the weather conditions.

Aretha could hear the voices get closer to her apartment.

Tomorrow I will finish mowing the lawn for my grandmother.

As the darkness fell in the evening, our group began to walk cautiously.

It is important to eat vegetables to have a balanced diet.

Eli slipped as he reached the upper limb of the oak tree.

The hardwood tree died due to gypsy moth infestation.

Many California homeowners have suffered in recent years because of forest fires.

Scientists have developed theories about why we remember dreams.

By not participating in tutorial sessions, Heather was barely succeeding in school.

The advanced students needed as much extra time to complete the algebra assignment as anyone else.

New research indicates that even high achieving students can lack confidence.

Sportive bikes are a more comfortable version of racing bikes.

More than 8 million metric tons of discarded plastic materials have become a menace to the earth's oceans.

The gluteus maximus is one of the posterior leg muscles in human beings.

Southeast Asia is comprised of various states between the Indian and Pacific oceans.

Many teens prefer young adult nonfiction texts over narrative selections.

Jim completed the learner's permit requirements on Thursday but barely passed the driver's test.

Silicon Valley is a region in California famous for the innovation and creativity of its workers.

Volcano is the name of a small village on the Big Island of Hawaii that has had as many as 800 earthquakes in one day.

Craftsmen sometimes use cypress for building Adirondack chairs since it does not require preservatives or other treatments.

NARRATIVE READING PASSAGES: WINTER TERM

Birthday at the Zoo

It was Sunday.

I got out of bed and went to eat.

Mom said, "Today is your birthday, Pat. What do you want to do?"

I wanted a party but I did not tell Mom.

I said, "I just want to play."

Mom said, "Come take a ride with me."

I got in the car and soon we were in the city.

The car stopped. We got out.

We walked past some trees and I saw a sign that said "City Zoo."

All my friends were at the gate.

I was all smiles. Mom had planned a party for me.

It was the best birthday ever.

Mary's New Bike

Mary wanted to get a new ten-speed bicycle. She helped with chores around the house to earn money. Mary had helped her father rake leaves and clean the apartment for extra money. But she still didn't have enough money to buy her new bike.

One day her Aunt Susan came to visit Mary's family. Aunt Susan heard that Mary wanted a new bike and told her she had a job for her. Mary walked over to Aunt Susan's house the very next day, ready to go to work.

Aunt Susan had Mary mop her kitchen floor and clean out the flowerbeds. Next, Mary swept out the carport. Finally, Aunt Susan asked Mary to fold her clean clothes. Mary was tired by the end of the day. But when Aunt Susan paid Mary her money, Mary smiled and hugged Aunt Susan. She hurried home to tell her parents the good news. They smiled and told her how proud they were.

The next day Mary went to the store and bought her new bicycle.

Bedtime

The sun was going down, the air was hot, and Wild Willie was afraid. Never had he been in such a dry, hot place in his long life. His horse named Wizard, once a wild Mustang he had caught and tamed, was searching for a few blades of grass to fill his empty stomach. Wild Willie was drowsy after many hours in the saddle, but sleep was not possible. Just then he heard the weird sound again—the same sound he had been hearing for days on his trek across the plains. What could it be and why was it following him? How could he find out what or who it was that was on his trail and drawing closer all the time?

Slowly Wizard turned around and Willie stood up in the stirrups to look over the distant sand dune. He saw no one, but once again he heard the bizarre and creepy sound. This time it came from behind where they stood and now made a low rumbling sound. He got off his horse. Gradually the sound came closer and closer. Willie looked up in terror and saw...

Just then the TV went blank and a voice said, "Beth, it's time to go to bed. Tomorrow is a school day and it's getting late." "Aw, Mom, can't I finish watching this TV show?" I asked. "No, you can record the show and watch it tomorrow afternoon after school," my mother replied.

As I went slowly upstairs to bed, I wondered what Wild Willie had seen. Maybe it had been some kind of creature, or perhaps just a person in a wagon. But it was probably the Ghost of the Sand Wind that caused terror in Wild Willie's heart. Yeah, that had to be the mysterious sound he heard. Other cowboys in the series claimed to have seen it, too. But I suppose I won't know until tomorrow.

A Different Time

Marlo lived in a different time and a different place many centuries ago. He lived in a time of darkness and gloom in a small hut with his poor parents. Marlo didn't have nice clothes to wear and he certainly didn't have much in the way of wholesome food to fill his stomach. However, the thing he wanted most, the opportunity to read, was not attainable. You see, the ruler would not allow any of his villagers to have books.

One day Marlo's father sent him to the castle with a cart of vegetables to sell to other peasants. Along the way Marlo met an old man who wore a hood over his head, but when he looked up his eyes were deep blue and sparkled. The old man asked Marlo if he could please have a few vegetables to eat because he was starving and had no money. Marlo agreed, even though he knew he would get into trouble, and gave the old one all he could eat. When the old man finally finished his meal he said, "Come to the old oak tree tonight and the future will be yours for the taking." Marlo walked away wondering what the old man meant.

That night when his family was asleep, Marlo slipped out of their tiny house and ran up the road until he reached the old oak tree. There he found the old man sitting on the ground holding a large box.

The old man stood up and handed the package to the boy. He said, "Marlo, inside this box is what you have always wanted.

Your life will never be the same." Marlo took the box and looked down at it for just a second, and when he looked up again the old man had vanished. Marlo rushed home and eagerly unwrapped the package, and there in the box Marlo discovered the greatest of gifts, a book.

Afternoon Walk

One day Allison was hiking in the woods alongside her house. Some of the teenagers in the neighborhood tried to frighten her by saying that the woods were haunted. "There's an old, withered, witch woman in those woods who makes children scrub her floors with toothbrushes, wash her smelly old garments by hand, and dig holes big enough to plant huge trees. Then, when the children are worn out, she sells them to a horrid-looking dwarf from Australia to work in the salt mines. Once captured they are never seen again, at least not in our country." Allison knew her friends were only telling stories, but it still frightened her sometimes when she went into the woods unescorted.

On this particular morning, Allison thought she would take a short stroll to find her mother's favorite wildflowers. Mother loved black-eyed Susans, vervains, bluebonnets and Indian Paintbrushes most of all. After walking for an hour or so, she stopped to rest under an elm tree. Unfortunately, she fell fast asleep. The next thing she knew, Allison was being shaken by a terribly unattractive old woman dressed all in black. Startled, Allison looked at her watch and saw it was already two o'clock. The old woman took Allison by the hand and led her to a run-down old hut.

For what seemed like hours, Allison had to wash dishes, clean out a doghouse, and scrub floors. While cleaning out the dog-house, she found a dog tag that read "Spirit." She tucked it into her pocket thinking she would give it to the woman later. The old woman checked on Allison every few minutes and always asked Allison if she were tired. Allison always said that she wasn't tired because she remembered the story of the dwarf.

It was just after Allison finished the doghouse that her chance to escape occurred. The old woman went into a back room calling for Spirit, so Allison quickly ran out the door. Allison ran and ran until she finally couldn't run any farther. She lay down under an elm tree and fell asleep.

Allison was awakened by her brother who said, "Mom says it's getting late and you'd better come home quick." Allison said, "You won't believe the horrible dream I just had." She told her brother all about it on their way home. All he said was, "Get serious."

Later that night when Allison was preparing for bed, a small metal tag fell from her pocket with "Spirit" printed on it.

Laser Boy

Matthew was a 13-year-old boy who never seemed to do well in school. Some thought he was a misfit or an outsider; someone who doesn't quite fit in with the other kids his age. Not only that, Matthew had trouble in school with his grades nearly his whole life. Sometimes he refused to complete his homework even when it was an easy assignment. In short, Matthew always seemed to struggle in school.

One day a concerned teacher decided to find out what Matthew's problem was in school. She arranged to have him tested and found out from the guidance counselor that Matthew was actually gifted in the areas of science and mathematics! "Oh, yes, sometimes students who do poorly in school are really quite gifted in certain areas, but just haven't had the opportunity to show what they can do. Also, gifted students are not always strong in academics, but may be talented in music, electrical or mechanical areas, or athletics."

After Matthew's special talents were known, his teachers asked what he was most interested in studying. Matthew answered that he found lasers to be fascinating and would like to learn about this technology. His science teacher arranged for Matthew to have permission to read everything he could find in the local university's library having to do with lasers. Later that same year, a professor in California was identified who was an expert on laser technology. The professor agreed to serve as his tutor on laser technology and visited with Matthew on a regular basis by phone.

During the last part of seventh grade, Matthew worked on a special science project for the annual science fair. He built a model laser that was accurate to the last detail. Everyone was impressed with his project and he won first place in the science fair competition. The kids at school were proud of their new science hero and he became known as "laser boy."

The Lawn Mower Business*

Mitchell was old enough now to work during summer vacation and earn his own money for the first time. Mitchell's uncle was retired from the landscaping business and offered to let him borrow his lawn mower and trimming equipment if he wanted to start his own summer business. Mitchell was thrilled to have the opportunity and thanked Uncle Jim for his kindness and generosity. That was the beginning of his lawn mower business.

One of the neighbors who hired Mitchell to mow her lawn every week was an older lady named Mrs. Luther. When Mitchell first met Mrs. Luther she said, "You look like you can handle the job, but how much do you charge?" Mitchell said, "For mowing a lawn your size and trimming the hedges, how about $30?"

Mrs. Luther responded, "Tell you what, Mitchell, if you were to do a perfect job, better than almost anyone could do, this would be a fifty-dollar lawn. But you would have to be the best in the world to earn fifty dollars. Here's what we will do, if you agree. Every time you mow and trim my yard you will be paid anywhere from twenty to forty dollars depending on how well the yard looks. How's that sound?"

Mitchell said, "That sounds fine, but I thought you said it was possible to earn fifty dollars, not forty dollars. Did you change your mind, Mrs. Luther?"

"Not at all," said Mrs. Luther, "I just know that it's almost impossible to mow a lawn that well. To answer your question, a fifty-dollar lawn is possible, just not likely you can mow a lawn on that level."

Week after week Mitchell worked his hardest trying to earn fifty dollars mowing Mrs. Luther's lawn. Two times that summer he earned forty dollars and was thrilled, but later that night he became frustrated. In the middle of the night following his most recent forty-dollar payday from Mrs. Luther, Mitchell awoke with a stark realization. He MUST find a way to do better and earn the fifty dollars Mrs. Luther said was impossible.

When the day arrived for Mrs. Luther's lawn to be mowed, Mitchell was out of bed at five o'clock in the morning. He prepared all his equipment, ate a decent breakfast, packed his water bottles to stay hydrated, and went to work. Instead of mowing the grass one time as usual, he mowed it two times in a checkerboard pattern. The result was spectacular, but he had only begun. Next, he trimmed the edges of the sidewalks with the weed eater and even trimmed along the house's foundation where weeds and grass were growing here and there.

Next on his list was trimming the hedges. For this task he got two long pieces of wood to use as stakes and tied a long string between them at the correct height for the hedges. Using a carpenter's level, he was able to make sure the string was perfectly level and straight. With the string as his guide he was able to trim the hedges to a perfect and consistent height.

His finishing touch was to use the leaf blower to gather all the cut grass and debris from mowing and trimming. The clippings were swept up and put in recycled bags and placed by the curb for pick-up by the city.

Mrs. Luther was shocked and amazed at the beauty of her lawn. Without hesitation she smiled and pulled a fifty-dollar bill from her purse and handed it to Mitchell. She said, "I got this brand new fifty-dollar bill from the bank the first day we talked. I knew you would earn it one day. Congratulations on a job well done... a fifty-dollar job!"

*Inspired by a true story told by Featherstone, V.J. (1975). *A generation of excellence: A guide for parents and youth leaders.* Salt Lake City, UT: Bookcraft.

Riley and Leonard

Looking back to his times in high school, Leonard recalled that he had felt like the most unpopular guy in school. No matter what he did to befriend his classmates, they constantly ridiculed Leonard and rejected his attempts at friendship. Perhaps it had been because he was small in stature, wore thick bifocal glasses, and didn't participate in extracurricular activities. Regardless of the possible motivations of his adolescent peers, Leonard had felt like a loser.

Leonard recalled a particular day back then when he was putting books in his locker. Several of his classmates had formed a semicircle around Leonard and began to taunt him and shout insults. Most of the assemblage had joined in after Riley McClure, an infamous bully at school, made Leonard drop his books. Leonard tried not to be provoked—that is, until Riley launched into a string of verbal abuses about Leonard's family and Leonard's mother in particular. Leonard became enraged and lunged at Riley, but Riley was much larger and more agile, so Leonard's attack quickly ended in disaster.

As the group finally disbanded, Lorrie Warner approached Leonard. Even though she had played no part in the hideous scene, she apologized for the group's behavior and tried to comfort Leonard's hurt pride. She said, "Just remember the old saying, *what goes around comes around*. Riley will get his due one day." But kind as she was, Lorrie's consoling remarks didn't assuage Leonard's bruised ego.

Twenty years after graduating from high school, Leonard found himself president of the largest bank in town. He was well respected in the community and was quite generous when it came to civic projects and charity work. Although he had not married at this point, he had recently begun dating his old classmate, Lorrie Warner.

One Friday evening, Leonard and Lorrie were dining at an elegant restaurant. They had finished their meal and were leaving when a beggar approached. The vagrant requested money to buy food and he did indeed appear to be famished. Looking into his eyes, Leonard noticed something familiar about the beggar that he could not quite place. Being the generous person he had become, Leonard gave the homeless person twenty dollars and wished him well. The beggar was so surprised by the large amount that he shook Leonard's hand vigorously before quickly disappearing down the street as fast as his legs could carry him. Lorrie shouted a word of caution to the beggar, but her warning came too late. The beggar had run into the path of a commercial truck and was struck down. After calling 911 for assistance, Leonard and Lorrie waited with the poor vagrant until an ambulance took him to the nearest hospital.

The next morning a local newspaper carried the story of a beggar who had been struck by a truck the previous night. He had died from internal injuries earlier that morning at the hospital. Leonard suddenly dropped the paper and turned pale when he learned the deceased beggar's name was Riley McClure.

A Long Night In The Big Easy

I arrived later than expected one October evening at the New Orleans International Airport due to weather delays in St. Louis. A call to my private investigations agency from a distraught lady named Ms. Killingsworth the previous week is what brought me to this town, known as The Big Easy and the Crescent City. Killingsworth said the matter was urgent and possibly dangerous, but that she could only share the details in person after my arrival and had already sent via overnight courier a five thousand dollar retainer for my services and a first-class nonstop airline ticket to New Orleans.

Night was descending as I took a taxi to the city center for the rendezvous with my client. As the cab made its way along the nearly deserted streets, the cabbie shared information with me about New Orleans and its traditions. She spoke with a languid Cajun accent common to the indigenous people of southern Louisiana, and her multicolored frock echoed the legendary and intriguing culture of the region. When I mentioned that I needed to go to a particular area of Rampart Street in the French Quarter, she seemed shocked and uneasy as she abruptly changed course and drove southwest.

Fifteen minutes later, and without another word uttered by my Cajun cabbie, I arrived at my destination and tipped her generously before making my way up Rampart Street. I was a few gloomy blocks away from all the merriment of the French Quarter that was brightly lit even at this late hour. I could hear the distant sounds of New Orleans jazz music pouring from the saloons and nightspots. After walking another two blocks, I noticed that a wretched little man was following me about 30 yards behind. I hesitate to say *wretched*, but his distressed face became visible as he passed under a gas streetlight and he appeared as if an unending series of cruel misfortunes had battered him throughout his life. The ogre's pace seemed to be matched to mine as I made my way up the dark and dank street searching for my client's residence. Whenever I stopped, he stopped; if I increased my speed, his pace quickened as well. Finally, I turned a corner and surreptitiously slipped into a concealed doorway. A few moments later, as the peculiar creature rounded the corner, I deftly reached out and grabbed him by his grimy coat.

"Why are you following me?" I demanded, but he only whimpered and eventually handed me a crumpled note. As my eyes scanned the message my grasp relaxed enough for him to slip away and the strange creature disappeared into an advancing fog bank. Could this note be a dispatch from my mysterious client?

I read the following message: "Your death is rapidly approaching. Run if you value your life." Needless to say, I didn't stand around pondering the possible subtle meanings of the message. No macho acts of bravery for me... I ran!

As I rounded the corner of Rampart and Royal I almost ran straight into a police officer. Feeling a measure of relief, I quickly told my story to the cop who, once I had finished my tale, seemingly thought I was either lying or insane. In the end he only chuckled and said, "Sure buddy, whatever you say. I suggest you go home and sleep it off." After he had walked away, I noticed a set of eyes from behind a recycling bin in the alleyway, so once again I ran for my life. Later I wondered if those eyes might have been from something as inoffensive as a cat, but you had to be there to know just how panicked I had become.

As I streaked through another alley, two huge, burly men seized me. "Nero" had sent them, they said, and they ordered me to reveal where I had put "the package." I told them I had no idea what they were referring to and said they had the wrong guy. Obviously thinking I was lying, they tied me up with rope and I was transported to a dingy building where my fate was to be decided.

As soon as my eyes adjusted to the glow and faint buzz of flickering fluorescent lights, I saw a man with a formidable belly sitting across from me at a table. He leaned forward and I could see his face, the face of pure evil. After studying me carefully for a full thirty seconds, he glanced at his goons with an exasperated expression. "You brought me the wrong man. This isn't Mouser, you idiots, get him out of here and make sure he never talks!"

I was blindfolded, led out of the building, and shoved into the trunk of a car. An hour later I was dumped headfirst into a deserted alleyway north of The Big Easy. The thugs left me tied up and blindfolded and said as they prepared to leave, "We're doing you a favor, bucko. Breathe a word of this to anyone and we'll be back to finish the job." That next morning, I left the Crescent City and, until now, have never told anyone about my experience. Maybe I need to consider another line of work.

FORM C

SPRING TERM
SENTENCES FOR INITIAL
PASSAGE SELECTION

NARRATIVE READING PASSAGES

SENTENCES FOR INITIAL PASSAGE SELECTION – SPRING TERM (S)*

FORM C

Mom told me to be quite careful with the baby.

New babies are very tiny and cry often.

Many families have more than one child.

Many people would rather live in apartments.

It is difficult to manage large pets in a city.

People in some large cities prefer to ride trains to get to work.

Unexpected loud noises can be rather frightening, especially at night.

Many children share a bedroom with their brothers or sisters.

I do not like to have to wake up during a vivid dream.

Taking risks can be rewarding, but also dangerous or unpredictable.

Almost all animal mothers will fiercely protect their young from any intruders.

Camping is one way to learn to appreciate the wonders of nature.

Holidays usually mean a festive and generally overflowing table at my house.

Roasted turkey is the typical main course at many traditional family gatherings.

Long languid weekends at home with family are my favorite winter times.

The seasonal flu can be severe and may include elevated temperature, chills, and a harsh cough.

When some people speak, it can be difficult to decide what is fact and what is fiction.

Many people dread Mondays when they have to again rise very early to prepare for work or school.

Men and women in some remote areas of the world have an average life expectancy of nearly 100 years.

We commemorate and honor the service and courage of veterans by decorating their graves with flags.

It is somewhat typical that people often fear places and things that are unfamiliar and foreign to their personal experiences.

The height you will attain as an adult is, in large part, governed by genetics, nutrition, and overall health during childhood.

We are increasingly influenced by the media in our attitudes and patterns of purchasing.

Often an empathetic friend can listen and help guide our responses in difficult or trying situations.

Some students have significant difficulty mastering tasks that require rote memorization, such as multiplication.

Mathematics ability is one of the most valid predictors of both high school and university academic success.

Even lifelong friends can have their relationship become strained or clearly tense in competitive situations.

NARRATIVE READING PASSAGES: SPRING TERM

Our New Baby

 What should we name the new baby? She was born just yesterday and was coming home tomorrow. Mom wanted to call the baby Mary because that was her mother's name. Dad said he thought Mary was a fine name, but he wanted to name the baby Grace. Spencer did not like those names at all. He thought and thought. What would be the very best name for his new little baby sister?

Dad took him to see Mom and the new baby at the hospital. His mom let him hold the new baby very carefully. The new baby was really tiny, and her face was very red. She looked right at Spencer and smiled. Mom told Spencer that his baby sister already knew her loving and kind big brother.

He felt such happiness that his mom and the baby were coming home tomorrow. Now he knew what the best name was for this sweet sister. Spencer told his mom and dad that they should call the baby Joy because she gave them joy. They all smiled. It was the perfect name!

Drake's Problem

Drake lived with his mother and elderly grandmother in an upstairs apartment of an old house. The house was located near the train station, making it easy for Drake's mom to travel to work.

Drake wanted a pet more than anything in the world. He would like any pet, even a pet mouse. But it seemed impossible. The manager who had rented the apartment to them had told them the rule. Absolutely no pets allowed.

One afternoon Drake observed a tiny chocolate-colored puppy just sitting on the curb next to a very crowded and busy street. He rushed to pick it up before it wandered in the street and was injured or killed by a car or bus.

But now Drake had a huge problem to solve. He could not bring the dog home, but he could not leave it there on the street. Drake walked and walked holding the little dog and wondering what to do next.

Finally, Drake got tired out from walking. He just sat on his front porch cuddling the puppy. The apartment manager came down the stairs and noticed him holding the dog. At first, the manager was quite angry to see a dog near the apartments. But then Drake told him the whole story about the puppy he had found in such danger.

The apartment manager smiled. He told Drake, "If the other people in the apartments do not complain, you have my permission to keep the puppy." Drake was thrilled. His good deed had saved the puppy and gave him his dearest wish – a pet!

What Was That Sound?

Jacob was in the middle of a great dream about a victory in the 100-meter race in P.E. Suddenly he heard an extremely loud noise and was startled awake. He did not want to be frightened but he certainly was. He pulled the worn quilt up around his face and neck and sat straight up in the bed. The room was now very silent except for the city sounds of the traffic coming from below.

Jacob's eyes began to get accustomed to the dark. He scanned around his bedroom, not seeing anything out of place. He glimpsed over to see his brother Josh was still sound asleep on the other bed. Jacob stayed in his bed. He was still a little too nervous to get out of bed to investigate.

Jacob began to wonder if he had only heard the noise in his dream. He lay back down, buried his head in his pillow, closed his eyes, and tried to return to that race dream. He heard the noise again. Sitting up, he saw the curtain rustle and the blind rattle. Now he was really freaked out.

Josh awoke and sat up this time. Jacob could see his little brother was petrified. They both looked at the window and were so surprised to see their pet parakeet, Oscar, flying right at the pane. Oscar had somehow gotten out of his cage. Both boys laughed and jumped out of their beds and began trying to catch their silly bird.

The Adventure Girl

Sloane was called "the adventure girl" by her parents. She did not seem to be afraid of anything whatsoever. Sloane climbed trees, swung high on the swings, and waded into icy streams.

Her mom said she actually climbed out of her crib before she was 1 year old.

One day, when the family was camping, Sloane had quite an experience. She was sitting on a log outside the tent as the sun was going down when she heard a sound like a kitten meowing very loudly. Sophie ran over to the side of the tent and saw what she thought was a furry black kitten. It was so cute that she reached out to cuddle it. But then she looked carefully at the chubby little animal and decided that it looked just like a baby black bear.

Indeed, it was a small young bear. Sloane thought it would be a real adventure to play with such a cute baby bear. But lucky for her she remembered that baby bears usually were not far from their mothers. That meant a big and probably not so cuddly bear was nearby.

Adventure girl Sloane gently pushed the baby bear back into the woods. She told her parents about the young visitor. They decided that their adventure girl needed a new name... Wise Sloane.

Thanksgiving

Logan glanced around the Thanksgiving tables and was thinking that this holiday was so predictable. It seemed that each year the same routines and patterns happened starting with Mom and Aunt Sara spending three days cleaning, cooking, and decorating the house. Then numerous family members and friends would come over to share the mountains of food and festivities.

He already knew what would happen next. Right after dinner, the usual groups of people would meet in different rooms to chat or to watch football. Some of the family typically wanted to shop the following weekend, so they would sit together looking at advertisements and plan their marathon shopping trips.

To be honest, kids were kind of in the way on Thanksgiving, or at least it seemed that way. They sat at a different table and had to amuse themselves while the adults ate, drank, and laughed in the other rooms. Logan was not complaining, but it seemed to him that this was an adult holiday and definitely not designed for kids.

Then he realized that something was quite different his year, and not in a good way. Uncle David was not at any table. His Mom had told him that Uncle David was in the Army overseas and could not make it home this year. At first, he had not thought it a big deal when she told him. But as he looked around today Logan saw that a piece of the family puzzle was missing, leaving him feeling weird and a little sad.

Logan got up from his seat and went into the kitchen where his mom was preparing extra food platters. He told her how he missed his funny Uncle David and how strange it was to have Thanksgiving without him. His mom stopped for a minute and hugged him tightly, and told Logan she knew exactly how he was feeling. "Family is the heart of Thanksgiving," she said, "and now clearly you are growing up and understand why family and loved ones being together is so important. We can only hope that Uncle David is with us next year. Until then we will cherish all the people who are here with us today." Logan now understood that this holiday was not just for adults. Thanksgiving celebrates everyone you love.

I Hate Mondays!

Every Sunday night my brother Adam would get ill, or at least that is what he reported to the family. Each Sunday, it was a different variety of ailment as well; sometimes it was his stomach and other times it was a headache or some other random body part that was causing him pain. He became very creative with his medical conditions and we never knew what disorder might appear each week. The family began describing it as Adam's Sunday illness report or "SIR" for short. Mom and Dad were not fooled by his vague and often outrageous medical misfortunes, as they seemed to understand that the early morning routine and rigid schedule of Mondays hit Adam hard.

One Sunday night, Adam was markedly quieter than usual with no SIR for a change. Mom went to his room to kiss him good night and noticed that he seemed warm and feverish and was clearly shivering under the quilt. She called out to dad to bring her the thermometer.

After finding out that Adam's fever was 103 degrees, Mom immediately put him in a bathtub of cool water and gave him some medication to quickly reduce the fever. On Monday, the doctor concluded that Adam had some sort of flu-like illness and he missed school both Monday and Tuesday to recuperate.

The whole family was puzzled by the fact that the one Sunday night he honestly *was* ill, Adam did not inform the family. Adam simply remarked that he did not think anyone would think he was credible because he had cried Wolf so many times before. We all had to agree with that conclusion.

I wish I could say my brother Adam had no more SIR events, but he did. They were fewer and did not occur every single Sunday, but he still hated Mondays!

The Cemetery

Cemeteries terrified and spooked Sydney. She did not even like to be a passenger in a car when driving past one. She would avert her eyes away from the cemetery and chant repetitively under her breath to keep her mind from focusing on the rows of tombstones that seemed to go on forever. Rationally, Sydney knew she was being ridiculous and obviously childish. But as long as she could remember, she had felt this cold dread at even seeing the word *cemetery*.

But one day she was forced to face her fears and trepidation when her Great-Uncle Donald died at age 96. He had served as an infantryman in the Second World War on the Italian front and had been quite clear that he was to be buried with his wartime comrades in a veteran's cemetery.

After a brief religious service, she and her family rode behind the hearse towards the cemetery. Sydney was astonished at the row after row of white crosses and tomb stones all honoring veterans of war and conflicts for which many had given their lives. As she walked to the gravesite, she looked at the names and dates inscribed on the simple markers. One of the men, Rudy Rizzardi, was only 8 years older than she was when he was killed in combat.

This experience dramatically changed Sydney's attitude towards cemeteries. She now realized that cemeteries and gravesites provided the living a place to remember and honor people who were loved or who gave their lives for others.

Being Herself

Whitney was simply a large person and had been larger than average since birth. She was definitely taller than any girl in her grade and considerably taller and heavier than most of the boys. It was rather difficult, especially for a female, to be constantly considered the big person in the crowd. Other students were continually making comments about her playing nose tackle or asking how the weather was up there. Whitney did not believe that the other students were attempting to offend her, as they probably considered their words friendly teasing or banter. Whitney typically acted like the jokes and rather snide remarks did not affect her, but if she were to be honest with herself, they were very wounding.

Not that there was much sympathy at home either. Whitney's mom was a large person as well, and simply did not believe that being larger than others presented any sort of dilemma. Dad believed Whitney strongly resembled her mother and, since he thought her mother was beautiful, Whitney was beautiful as well.

Whitney felt that small petite girls had a significant physical advantage over larger girls; certainly, the women and girls in magazines and on television were absolutely tiny compared to her. She felt as if she were the size of a hulking lumberjack sometimes when she walked in the halls near the other girls at school.

A teacher at school, Mrs. Strauss, noticed that Whitney was slumping while she walked and asked to confer with her after school. Knowing Mrs. Strauss could be a trusted confidante, Whitney admitted that she was literally trying to appear smaller and thought perhaps if she hunched over a little when she walked she would appear more like the other girls in stature.

Mrs. Strauss listened intently to Whitney and emphasized to her that this world needs more strong and powerful women who walk tall and are proud to be themselves, whatever their size. The old adage that beauty is only skin-deep sounds trite, but as Mrs. Strauss reminded Whitney, a person is so much more than simply her height or weight. "Listen to your father," she suggested. "You are beautiful... embrace your personal beauty."

Whitney left feeling somewhat better, although it was still difficult to be the big one in a world that celebrates female physical beauty so obviously. Whitney felt affirmed by Mrs. Strauss and decided no more hunching over for her and, additionally, she no longer was going to take to heart comments by others. Just like her Dad said, she was beautiful.

Always Together

Seth and Sean had been inseparable since the day their parents had enrolled them in preschool. While their parents completed paperwork for admission, the boys met at the turtle-shaped sandbox and began throwing sand at one another. As their parents intervened, the boys started giggling and a friendship was cemented.

Not only did their first names start with the same letter, their last names were identical, Smith. So, invariably, they sat together in almost every school function in which the students were seated in alphabetical order. These similarities caused many humorous situations. It was not uncommon for teachers to confuse them, although the boys were nothing alike in appearance.

In eighth grade, it became obvious that Sean was having difficulty mastering algebra. He simply could not memorize the algorithms, despite determined effort and intense tutoring, but this lack of skill proved to be a considerable barrier, slowing his school performance and frustrating him greatly. Seth sympathized with Sean, but did not understand his friend's quandary as algebra was not difficult for him; Seth could rattle off the algorithms with ease and without hesitation.

Seth pondered how he could assist Sean to learn algebra as he feared that the two boys would eventually be grouped differently if he continued to fall behind. That was unacceptable to both of them, so a plan was devised.

Sean had been reading some science journals about how to utilize music to enable learning of some skills. He shared with Seth that music activated large-scale neural networks in the brain in ways that simple speech does not. Using this information,

Seth and Sean created a rap with all the basic algebra algorithms as lyrics, hoping that with practice, perhaps Sean would memorize the rap.

Their plan worked seamlessly as the boys created a rap that was so rhythmic and unforgettable that Sean learned the facts almost without effort. The rap was so catchy that Sean and Seth were asked to perform it for their class to resounding applause.

FORM
D

FALL TERM EXPOSITORY
READING PASSAGES

SENTENCES FOR INITIAL PASSAGE SELECTION: FALL TERM (F)

FORM

D

Some animals are fun.

I eat lots of food.

He can smell good.

It was a very clear night in the swamp.

I get hot when the sun shines on me during summer.

We cannot see air moving.

There are insects that can be very helpful to farm animals.

Some adults are slender, while others can be plump.

I think that roses are among the most beautiful flowers.

A smart person would know what to do in this dire situation.

The invention was very important to the global steel industry.

Marty likes syrup on her waffles for breakfast.

Randy took his automobile to the shop, but the estimate for repairs was not acceptable.

Various authorities came to inspect the disaster scene.

Knowing how much water to drink each day is critical to your health.

Steven considered the organization's proposal carefully, but decided to decline the offer.

Global warming is causing ocean levels to rise on every continent.

What is common today in medical procedures is the direct result of many years of research.

A canine tooth is also known as a cuspid or eye tooth in mammals.

All matter in the universe is comprised of the atoms of at least 100 chemical elements.

Most gemstones receive their colors from impurities in their structure.

The friction of ash rushing upward in the crater creates volcanic lightning.

Fiber optics technicians handle installations and maintain systems in businesses.

Performing musicians usually have a portable public address system, also known as a P. A.

Moving objects undergo acceleration caused by centripetal force when moving in a circular motion.

Acts betraying or trying to overthrow the government of one's country is the crime known as treason.

Monologues in theater productions of Shakespeare's works are sometimes referred to as a soliloquy.

Dogs

Dogs are our pets.

Dogs are many colors.

Some dogs are brown.

Others are black.

There are white dogs too.

Many dogs are big.

Some dogs are little.

Dogs have big teeth.

Some dogs have big ears.

Dogs can run fast.

Some dogs swim.

Dogs like to play.

Some dogs like cats.

Dogs like to eat.

Dogs eat meat.

Some dogs eat shoes!

Dogs are fun!

Bright Stars

Look up at the sky at night. If it is a clear night you will see stars. How many stars are there? No one knows for sure. But there is one star that you know by name. You can see it in the daytime. It is our Sun.

The Sun is a type of star. All stars are suns. Our sun is very close and so bright that we cannot see the other stars in the daylight. We only can see them at night.

Stars are made up of very hot gases, and they appear to twinkle because of the winds moving across them. Even though we cannot see them, they are always in the sky, even in the daytime.

Flying Flowers

Our planet has many types of insects. For example, there are ants, bees, grasshoppers, cockroaches, and wasps. But there is one species that most people agree is the most beautiful and has been called the "flying flower." It is the butterfly.

Butterflies are insects that have two pairs of wings. Their wings are covered with different tinted scales that cause its beautiful colors. Butterflies smell and hear by using their long, thin antennae. Butterflies use long tube-like tongues to reach the food they need from flowers.

Butterflies begin as eggs and then hatch into caterpillars. A caterpillar forms a hard skin called a chrysalis. When they finally break out of the hard skin, they have become butterflies. Adult butterflies must lay eggs soon because they do not live very long.

Butterflies and moths are different. Butterflies like the day, but moths prefer night. Some moths are just as colorful as butterflies. Butterfly bodies are slender, but moths tend to have large, fat bodies. Moths form cocoons before turning into winged insects.

The Story of Coca-Cola

Coca-Cola is a world-famous soft drink. But not many people know the real story about how this drink was created. It was the invention of John Pemberton in 1886. Although he wasn't a medical doctor, most people called him Doctor Pemberton. He was a chemist and inventor who also owned several drug stores.

One day he decided to invent a headache medicine. It was made from nuts, fruits, and leaves. He also added a drug necessary to cure a headache. Doctor Pemberton took a jug of the syrup to one of his drugstores. He told the manager to mix it with water for people with headaches. At first it did not sell very well.

One day a clerk sold the new drink to a customer with a bad headache. He accidentally used carbonated water instead of regular water. Customers loved this new change to the drink. Later, the medicine was removed from Coca-Cola. It continues to be one of the world's most popular drinks.

Popcorn

There are three main types of corn grown in the United States. First, there is the common type of corn people eat as a vegetable. It is known as sweet corn because of its flavor. Second is field corn, used mainly for feeding livestock. Many people eat field corn, too. However, its taste is not as sweet, and the kernels are smaller. The third type of corn is often called Indian corn or popcorn. The average American eats almost 68 quarts of popcorn each year.

Native Americans have enjoyed popcorn for thousands of years. They used to prepare it several different ways. One method was to place an ear of corn on a stick and hold it over a campfire. Any kernels that popped out of the fire were gathered and consumed. Another approach was to scrape the cob and throw kernels into the fire. Kernels popping clear of the fire were immediately eaten. Native Americans began to use small clay bowls that they would heat in sand. When the sand grew hot enough, they placed the popcorn into the bowls and waited for the kernels to pop.

Corn pops because of the amount of water content. Kernels should contain at least fourteen percent water for popping. If corn has less than twelve percent water content the kernels will fail to pop.

Careers In Cooking

Numerous people choose careers in cooking. Known as the culinary arts, there are myriad fields one may choose. Restaurant occupations alone are expected to grow twelve percent per year through 2026. Here are some of the areas people are considering.

Chefs are food preparers who often serve as head cook in a restaurant. Getting a culinary arts education is a good place to start if one's goal is to open a coffee shop or become top chef. Learning from successful professionals provides a basic foundation for getting started. Years of experience will lead to greater knowledge and skill in food preparation.

Restaurant managers handle the business side of the industry. This is an ideal position for people who want to supervise talented people and run a business. Managers are involved with hiring, training, and supporting great people. Employees hired fill such roles as wait staff, cooks, custodial crew, and food buyers.

Other careers have emerged in recent decades for the culinary arts that many are considering. These include bed and breakfast ownership, hospitality manager, and cookbook author. One of the more unique options is professional food forager. This is a person who locates locally grown food ingredients and farm products. Some foragers go into wilderness areas to collect ingredients for restaurants. These include wild berries, bamboo shoots, mushrooms, and nettles.

Diamonds

A diamond is one of the most exquisite treasures found in nature. It takes thousands of years for nature to transform a chunk of carbon into a rough diamond. India, South America, and Africa are home to the three primary mining fields in the world producing high quality diamonds.

The rock in which diamonds are found is called *blue ground*. The first diamonds, called *alluvial diamonds,* were found in streambeds. Diamonds are also found deep in the earth in rock formations called *pipes.* It takes sorting through tons of rock to find enough diamonds for a one-carat ring.

Diamonds are sometimes mined and sold for criminal purposes. Blood Diamonds, also known as Conflict Diamonds, are those produced through the slave labor of adults and children by criminals. Blood Diamonds are sold as gemstones around the world and the money used to buy weapons for rebel military actions. Blood Diamonds come from such areas as Angola, Congo, Sierra Leone, and the Ivory Coast. The movie *Blood Diamond* is a fictional account set in the 1990s. It describes how Conflict Diamonds eventually find their way to jewelry stores alongside legally produced gems.

For diamonds to be considered gem quality they must be graded according to weight, purity, color, and cut. *Carat* is the unit of measure for the weight of a diamond. Diamond purity is determined by the amount of impurities, such as foreign minerals and uncrystallized carbon. Colors vary, but most diamonds are tinged yellow or brown. The cut of a diamond also figures into its value. A fully cut diamond, often called flawless, has fifty-eight facets. Facets, or sides, cause the brilliance that is produced when a diamond is struck by light.

Reversing Global Warming

Signs of global warming are all around us. Sea levels are slowly rising, and glaciers and polar ice packs are melting. The "greenhouse effect" is the source of global warming. This is what happens when certain gases like carbon dioxide accumulate in the Earth's atmosphere. Like the glass walls of a greenhouse, light gets through, but heat is trapped. The more greenhouse gases added to the atmosphere the hotter the Earth becomes. Scientists have known since 1895 that human beings make the greenhouse effect worse by adding carbon dioxide and other gases to the atmosphere. How bad is the problem? Greenhouse gases are at the highest level than in the last 650,000 years. This is a problem because the climate is changing at a rate quicker than living things can adapt.

There are several ways we can begin reversing global warming. Efficiency and conservation are excellent places to begin the effort. Since automobiles and other fossil-fueled machinery are primary causes of greenhouse gases, doubling their fuel economy would help reduce air pollution. Decreasing our reliance on cars through greater use of mass transit would also help the planet's health. Improving the efficiency of buildings by using energy efficient lights and air conditioning systems would also help. Greater use of wind and solar power, as well as natural gas, is likewise critical.

Solving complicated problems requires complicated solutions and reversing global warming is no exception. A multi-layered approach is required involving conservation, use of clean technologies, replanting and protecting forests, and smart use of natural resources. Together we can create a healthier planet.

Visual Illusions

A visual illusion, sometimes called a cognitive illusion, is a perception of visual information that differs from what is reality. You are confident you see something accurately and wholly, but in truth you do not. Your eyes (and the brain's visual cortex) can fool you. The visual cortex of the brain located in the occipital lobe located near the back of the brain actually is the sight organ in charge. Illusions occur when the brain unconsciously fills in visual gaps with what it expects to see based on past visual experiences. The connection between the brain and our visual system is complex in other ways as well. In other instances, an illusion is caused by the brain's difficulty in choosing from two or more visual patterns for processing.

If you look at a bull's-eye and move it slowly in circular motions, you are likely to see spokes moving as if in wheel movement. The spokes, if you see them, aren't really there. This type of visual illusion is called lateral inhibition.

Another type of visual illusion occurs when a person attempts to estimate the height of a vertical object. This very common illusion is referred to as length distortion. The famous Gateway Arch in Saint Louis, Missouri, is a commonly used example of length distortion because the arch appears for most viewers to be markedly higher than it is wide. In reality, the height and width of the arch are virtually identical. Length distortion occurs because our eyes move more easily from side to side than up and down. The greater muscular effort it takes the eyes to look up causes the brain to over-interpret the height of vertical objects.

If you look at a series of squares in a grid formation, you may see small gray spots at each intersection. However, if you look directly at only one intersection, the spots usually disappear. This illusion is known as Hermann's Grid. It can often be seen in modern high-rise office buildings when windows are separated by evenly placed strips of concrete creating a series of identical squares. These window patterns create the illusion and add to the visual interest of onlookers.

The above are only three examples of the many ways our eyes can deceive us. There are literally books filled with optical illusions that test our eye–brain connection and our patience! But they do reinforce the old axiom, "Don't believe everything you see."

FORM

E

WINTER TERM (W)

SENTENCES FOR INITIAL PASSAGE SELECTION: WINTER TERM (W)

FORM E

Dogs bark to tell us something.

Sometimes they are afraid.

Other times pups seem lonely.

Look at the objects found in your bedroom.

Did you notice that they all have shape, size, and color?

Purple is created by blending blue and red tints.

Gene likes books about agriculture.

An affordable flying car has not yet been invented.

Sea levels are rising due to climate change.

Lewis and Clark began their expedition in 1804.

President Jefferson asked them to explore land west of the Mississippi River.

Their excursion took them over 8000 miles and lasted over two years.

Mexico City is a fabulous destination for tourists.

The Palace of Fine Arts is the home of the Folk Ballet of Mexico.

Constitution Square, known as the Zocalo, is the location of the Governmental Palace.

Laws have been created to protect people against discrimination.

Employers may not differentiate in hiring based on race, gender, and religion.

Other forms of discrimination now prohibited by law include national origin, pregnancy, and disabilities.

There are forms of measurement everyone should know as an educated person.

Temperature is typically measured using the Fahrenheit and Celsius scales.

Celsius or Centigrade is the metric standard worldwide, except in the U.S., and zero degrees is the freezing point for water.

The North American continent has a great deal of ethnic, racial, economic, political, and religious diversity.

New Jersey, Texas, Maryland, and California are among the most diverse states in terms of racial groups.

The Census Bureau forecasts that the United States will become majority–minority by 2043.

Cholesterol is a waxy substance that is not inherently bad for your blood pressure.

Your body needs it to build cells, but too much can cause heart problems.

Foods high in saturated fats like meat, poultry, and full-fat dairy products can cause your liver to make more cholesterol than normal.

EXPOSITORY
READING PASSAGES
WINTER TERM (W)

FORM
E

Animal Friends

There are many different kinds of animals.

Some animals are our friends. Others are not.

Dogs and cats can be very good friends to people.

Dogs and cats make different sounds to talk to us.

Most dogs bark when they hear noises.

Some dogs bark when they are hungry.

Cats purr when they feel happy and loved.

Cats meow when they are hungry.

Not all cats and dogs are your friends.

If you do not know a dog, do not try to pet it.

It might not be friendly.

Cats can hurt you too.

Cats have claws and they can bite.

Art is Everywhere

Believe it or not, art is everywhere in our world – even in your own bedroom. Just look very carefully at all the objects around you. You will see that they all have lines, shape, and usually color. Artists use lines, shape, and color to make pictures, designs, and the things around us we see every day.

Lines can be thick or thin, short or long, curved or straight. Most artists and designers start with drawing lines as they plan their art. Lines are used to create many shapes. There are many different shapes in the objects you see.

Most objects also have color. Red, yellow, and blue are the main or primary colors. All other colors can be made by combining or mixing these colors. Orange is a mixture of red and yellow. Green is a mixture of yellow and blue. Purple is a mixture of red and blue. Black and white are not colors at all. Color is absent in black and white. Black and white do not have any blue, yellow, or red in them.

The History of Books

The history of books is fascinating. A long time ago most people could not read. The people who could read had very few books to read. They didn't have many books because the printing press had not yet been invented. The books had to be handwritten on either an animal skin or a kind of rough paper.

Most books were written on stretched sheepskin. The books were written on skins because the skins were stronger than the books written on paper. Hundreds of years ago it could have taken a whole flock of sheep to make one book because it took one sheepskin for each page.

The cost of writing a book on skin limited how many could be made. Books were very rare and costly. Only rich people could own books.

The invention of the printing press changed the world. The printing press allowed many more books to be made quickly. As books became more available, many more people began to learn how to read. For the first time, books began to be used to teach people about art, science, and faraway places. Books opened up the world.

Mountain Man

The Wild West was more than cowboys and American Indians. There was another group in the West called the mountain men. These tough men trapped animals, often beavers, for their furs. Then they sold the furs they collected for clothing and goods. The men lived outdoors in all kinds of rough weather. They usually carried a gun, a knife, coffee, flour, and little else. They ate the animals they shot for food. It was a dangerous life. The mountain men shared hunting territory with the American Indians. Some of the men were friendly with the American Indians. One famous mountain man who was a loved friend of the American Indians was Jim Beckwourth.

Jim Beckwourth was a black man who had been a slave. At the age of 20, he ran away from his slave master and escaped to the Rocky Mountains. There he became a very successful fur trapper. Jim became close friends with an American Indian tribe called the Crow. Later Jim married an American Indian woman and even became a chief of the Crows. But Jim was a mountain man who still had the wandering spirit. He wanted to explore even more and headed off for California. On his way, Jim discovered a pass through the mountains to California. That pass through the mountains still bears his name today. Jim Beckwourth couldn't read or write himself, but lucky for us, his story of adventure is told in a book called *The Life and Adventures of James P. Beckwourth.*

Music of Mexico

Much of the music you hear in the United States comes from other countries. Most people who come to the United States from other countries adapt to the lifestyle here. However, they do not give up the music of their homelands.

Many people have come to the United States from Mexico. Mexico is a large country that lies south of the United States. The music of Mexico is unique. Music from Mexico often uses instruments, such as the folk harp, violin, and various types of guitars.

Music in Mexico is used to celebrate birthdays, weddings, anniversaries, and other holidays. The people like music and they show it. They sing along with the musicians and often burst out with yells, laughter, clapping, and dancing.

Two types of music that are popular throughout Mexico are from states in the east and west. In the east, music is performed on four instruments. A band in the east generally has a 35-string harp that plays the melody and bass, a thin guitar, a six-string guitar, and a four-string guitar. The music is lively and fast paced. A famous song from this part of Mexico is "La Bamba." Music from the western part of Mexico is usually played by a musical group. These musical groups, called "mariachi" (mah-ree-AH-chee), play many types of music. The group usually consists of violins, two trumpets, a large bass guitar, a short five-string guitar, and a six-string guitar. Mariachi often played for special events. Other times, mariachi can be seen strolling along the street playing and singing to people eating or shopping.

Jesse Owens

In 1936, the Olympic games were to be held in Germany. Before the games took place, American people argued that the U.S. team should not attend. Germany was ruled by Adolf Hitler and the Nazi Party. Hitler had been mistreating German Jews for some time. Many people in the United States thought we should stay home as a protest. However, it was finally decided to send a team to the games. At the same time, many black athletes wondered about participating. There was much racism towards black Americans in the United States as well. Led by Jesse Owens, the black American athletes decided they should attend. They wanted to show the world their tremendous skills. Jesse Owens led the American team by capturing four Gold Medals. He returned home a national hero and many cities held parades and celebrations in his honor.

In his later life, Jesse Owens, without bitterness, wrote the following. "In the early 1830s, my ancestors were brought on a boat across the Atlantic Ocean from Africa to America as slaves for men who felt they had the right to own other men. In August of 1936, I boarded a boat to go back across the Atlantic Ocean to do battle with Adolf Hitler, a man who thought all other men should be slave to him and his armies."

Jesse Owens's Gold Medals did little to stop Germany in 1936. However, Jesse's courage did help move the United States a small step closer toward equal treatment.

Nails: A Carpenter's "Fastener"

Carpenters use many tools in their profession, such as hammers, saws, and power tools. They also use what are called *fasteners* to hold pieces of wood and other materials together. The most widely used fasteners are nails, screws, and bolts. Nails are the most commonly used fasteners in the carpenter's toolbox.

There are hundreds of kinds of nails that can be used for just about any kind of fastening job. The size of nails is described using the *penny system*. Many people believe that the penny system came from an ancient measurement based on the price of nails according to weight per one hundred nails. Larger and heavier nails would cost more pennies than smaller nails, so a six-penny nail (written as "6d") would cost more than a two-penny (2d) nail. In the penny system, the smallest nail is a two-penny (2d) nail and the largest is a sixty-penny (60d) nail. The thickness or *gauge* of nails increases as nails get longer, so a 50d nail will be much thicker in gauge than a 10d nail.

There are many ways of making nails, and each type is suited to different purposes. One type of nail that is not used very often is called the *cut* nail. Cut nails are given that name because they are literally cut or *stamped* from thin metal sheets.

Wire nails are cut from long rolls of metal wire and come in three types: common, box, and finish nails. *Common nails* have a smooth shaft, are of fairly heavy gauge, and have a medium-sized head. They may have a pointed or barbed section under the head to improve holding power. *Box nails* are much like common nails except they are much thinner (smaller gauge). This makes them better suited to fastening edges with less danger of splitting the wood. *Finish nails* are light gauge (very thin) and are ideal for what is called "finishing work" on the inside of homes. They have a small head and are difficult to see once hammered into wood.

An old saying among carpenters is "always use the right tool for the right job." Knowing just which nail is best for the job is one way of doing that.

The Environments of Africa

Africa is the Earth's second largest continent and home to about one-tenth of the world's population. While it is about three times larger than the United States in terms of landmass, many people still do not know very much about it. Some think of Africa as a single country or consider all Africans as being similar to one another. Both of these beliefs are false. Let's learn a little in this selection as we take a very brief tour of this continent.

Africa is almost completely surrounded by water. Two oceans and two seas are on its borders. The Atlantic Ocean borders Africa on the west, while the Indian Ocean borders to the east. The Mediterranean Sea and the Red Sea are to the north. The famous Sahara Desert stretches across Africa. It separates North African countries from the southern countries, which are often called sub-Saharan Africa. As of the 1990s, there were some 49 countries in sub-Saharan Africa alone. Because the equator runs through sub-Saharan Africa, most of this region has a climate that is quite warm and moist or *tropical*.

Central and West African countries are thinly populated because of a lack of suitable soil for farming. They do, however, have many tropical rain forests, which are of great benefit to people around the Earth. A major concern to many is that these splendid rain forests are being cut down to make way for farming and houses. Among other things, the loss of the rain forests leads to a great deal of soil erosion and the loss of plant and many animal habitats.

As we move further away from the equator, we find that the African rain forests disappear and are replaced by grasslands known as *savannas*. In East Africa, there are thick grasslands where large herds of big game animals, such as the giraffe, antelope, and zebra, roam. Farming is also an important way of life in these East Africa countries.

The *African Horn* is also part of East Africa and bulges out into the Indian Ocean. It is a mass of hills, mountains, canyons, and valleys that slope down toward the dry lowlands near the Red Sea. Because of overpopulation and other societal problems, there is a great deal of poverty in this region. The African Horn is home to four countries: Ethiopia, Somalia, Eritrea, and Djibouti.

Southern Africa is a fascinating place that features wooded areas to the north and, due to less rainfall, grasslands to the south. Some of the countries located in Southern Africa include Angola, Zambia, Namibia, and South Africa. There has been a great deal of political change in South Africa over the last twenty years as this country moved from government ruled by white citizens only to a democracy that allows everyone to vote for her leaders.

Finally, as we travel to North Africa above the Sahara Desert, we see that it is home to such ancient countries as Egypt, Sudan, Libya, Algeria, and Morocco. These nations have their own special character and traditions that can vary greatly from their African neighbors to the south. Without doubt, Africa is a continent rich in traditions, culture, and varied geography.

The Mathematics of Health

Americans spend billions of dollars every year on medical care. Doctor bills, medicine, dental work, glasses, health insurance, nursing homes, and other health-related costs are all part of the healthcare picture. As the costs of medical care continue to climb, more and more Americans are making efforts to stay healthy in many varied ways. These efforts range from daily exercise to careful control of one's diet. This passage will focus on the mathematics involved in monitoring one's diet.

People sometimes try to remain healthy by limiting the amount of fat, sodium (salt), cholesterol, and sugar in their diet. Too much fat in your diet, for instance, can lead to heart disease and other health problems. Years ago, many food producers began marketing products carrying labels like "LITE" (low in fat or sugar) or "Lo-Cal" (low in calories) to suggest that their foods were healthier than some of their competitors' products. Sometimes, however, these food products were not healthier than their competitors that did not carry the "LITE" or "Lo-Cal" markings.

In 1994, the federal Food and Drug Administration (FDA) in Washington, D.C., created new rules for food producers marking their products "LITE," "Lo-Cal," or "Light." Now all companies, except for the very smallest, must provide nutritional information on their labels. This enables consumers to judge for ourselves whether the food is low in fat, sodium, cholesterol, or sugar.

Sometimes when we are shopping for groceries, it can be interesting to compare products just to see how much fat is contained in them. This can help us to choose foods that are as healthy as they are

FORM E Winter Term (W)

pleasing to the taste. For example, a frankfurter typically has about thirteen grams of fat. (*Note:* This is written as "13 g" on the label next to where it says "Fat.") Roast turkey, on the other hand, has 12.5 g *less* fat than a frankfurter! Here is another example. A can of orange soda has about 110 calories, mostly due to the amount of sugar it contains. However, a LITE or diet soda only has about one calorie. If a grown person should usually consume about 1500 calories per day from all foods, think of how many calories can be saved for other more pleasing foods just by switching to a diet soda without sugar.

Becoming a "label reader" can be a great way to add years to your life, while also helping you enjoy the foods you eat. Maybe, as the old saying goes, "You *can* have your cake and eat it, too!" as long as you pay close attention to *what* you put into the cake.

STUDENT BOOKLET

EXPOSITORY PLACEMENT SENTENCES & EXPOSITORY READING PASSAGES

FORM

F

SPRING TERM (S)

SENTENCES FOR INITIAL PASSAGE SELECTION:
Spring Term (S)

All children should learn to swim.

It is fun to learn to float in water and blow bubbles.

Kicking is a part of swimming.

Did you know the first bicycles were made about 200 years ago?

The hobby horse or running machine was wooden and didn't have pedals.

High wheelers were the first bicycle, but were hard to mount and dangerous to ride.

Walking is almost as good a workout as running.

It is easier on joints and can improve mental health and fitness.

People can walk about one mile in twenty minutes and feel better, too.

Boats come in different sizes and serve different purposes.

Tugboats help ships coming into sea ports arrive safely.

Families on vacation sometimes rent pontoon boats.

The history of books began about 3500 years ago with the creation of portable stone tablets.

It was necessary to create an alphabet so that spoken words could be recorded.

Paper was first invented in China about two thousand years ago and each sheet was known as a leaf.

NASA hopes to have people colonizing the planet Mars by the year 2030.

Space travel over extensive distances over time carries a unique set of health problems.

Immune system issues, reduction in muscle mass, and visual problems are possibilities.

Statistics is a branch of mathematics used for collecting, analyzing, and interpreting masses of data.

Entrepreneurs use statistics to apprehend a population's needs prior to opening a business.

Other fields using numerical analysis include medicine, economics, aeronautics, and agriculture.

The Supreme Court has had to settle boundary disputes between states over many decades.

Pennsylvania and Maryland are two of the few to not quarrel over state lines after their ratification of the Mason-Dixon line as their common boundary.

Border disputes have happened historically between the United States and Mexico, as well as Great Britain.

Creative writing careers are available in myriad professions, but be prepared to pay your dues for low wages.

Once you have earned your college degree, perhaps consider becoming a literary consultant.

This combines publishing astuteness with composition skills to serve as a mentor for new and aspiring authors.

EXPOSITORY READING PASSAGES (S)

Dreams

When we sleep, we dream. Some of our dreams are funny and some of our dreams are a little scary. Many times, we dream about things that we do at home or at school. Sometimes we dream about our pets, our friends, or our family. If we watch a TV program, we can dream about that, too.

At night, sometimes, dreams wake us up. We think that it is real, but it is not. If you turn on the light and look around, you know that it was just a dream. That light helps if the dream is a little scary.

Do you tell your family about your dreams? Many children try to remember their dreams, but they forget! The best time to tell your family about your dreams is first thing in the morning before you get too busy.

Malala

A girl named Malala loved school very much. She liked learning and being with her friends. But in her country, the leaders made a new law–no girls could go to school. That shocked Malala and her family.

Malala wrote a speech about the importance of school. She was angry that girls were treated so poorly in her country. She spoke often to large crowds. Many people paid a great deal of attention to her speeches and podcasts. The leaders were very upset that such a little girl would be so brave against them. Malala's family had to leave their home. They were frightened that they would be punished by the leaders.

The leaders tried to hurt Malala, but it did not work. She recovered and wrote a book about how important it is for girls and boys to attend school.

The whole world began to love her and be amazed at her courage and strength. Malala was awarded an important prize – the Nobel Peace Prize. She is the youngest person ever to get this award. Malala still loves education and continues to speak up for all children to attend school and learn. She shows us how just one person can change the world.

Twins

Sometimes when babies are born, the mom and dad get a baby bonus because instead of just one baby being born, they get twins! Sonograms, which are much like safe x-rays, inform a pregnant mother that she is going to have twins. Knowing this helps the family plan ahead for the two new children.

Twins can be girl–girl, girl–boy or boy–boy sets. Many times, twin babies start out smaller than other babies because both of them had to share the mom's body. Some twin sets are born prematurely, or early. The smallest babies need to stay for a while in the hospital to gain weight or strength. Fortunately, even the tiniest twins become healthy and strong.

When twins are identical, they look almost exactly the same. Girl–girl twins can be identical and boy–boy twins can be identical. The babies can be so alike in face and body that their own moms and dads actually have to find a way not to confuse them. In one family, one baby girl always wore a red ribbon while her identical twin sister wore a blue ribbon.

Twins who are not identical are called fraternal twins who may or may not look alike. Some twins do not look alike at all. Obviously boy–girl twins look different, particularly after they begin to grow.

Even though they may look alike, twins have very different personalities from one another. Twins are unique individuals who share many experiences. Most twins enjoy being twins and having a built-in friend.

Mustangs

Mustangs are descendants of Spanish horses that were brought to the Americas in the 16th century. The word mustang comes from the Spanish word mustengo, which means "ownerless beast" or "stray horse."

Mustangs are a medium-sized horse. They measure about 56–60 inches tall. Most mustangs weigh around 800 pounds. Mustangs have a wide variety of colors, patches, spots, and stripes.

Most mustangs live in the grassland and prairie areas of the western United States. Some also live on the Atlantic coastal islands. The horses are allowed to run free on 34 million acres of public land. The number of mustangs has been steadily decreasing. Now, there are fewer than 25,000 mustangs left in the wild. This is most probably due to grasslands being developed for human use.

Mustangs live in large herds consisting of one stallion, around eight females, and their colts. The leaders of the herd are a female horse, or mare, and a stallion. When in danger, the head mare will lead her herd away to safety. The stallion will stay behind to defend or fight.

The wild mustangs' main diet is grass. Herds spend most of their time grazing on grasses, but they do play or snuggle together for a nap. Sometimes, when it looks like they are fighting, the young mustangs are actually playing together.

Valentine's Day

How did Valentine's Day become a special day to demonstrate love and friendship? Why do we celebrate this day by giving tokens of love and care to others? Valentine's Day started centuries ago in the ancient Roman Empire. People observed a holiday on February 14th to honor Juno – who is the Queen of Roman Gods and Goddesses as well as the Goddess of Women and Marriage. This was the beginning of a yearly pagan festival.

One of the stories about how this festival became Valentine's Day is that a man, who was called Valentine, began marrying people against the wishes of the ruler Emperor Claudius. Men had refused to join the army, not wanting to leave their wives and children. In response to their refusal, Claudius outlawed marriages. Claudius became very angry at Valentine and had him murdered. His death shocked and outraged the people. We really do not know if this story is true, but St. Valentine became a hero to people who believe in love and caring.

Valentine's Day is a very popular holiday all around the world. Over time, Valentine's Day became a day that celebrates love of all kinds, and not just romantic love. Today, Valentine's Day cards are given to teachers, parents, friends, siblings, and sweethearts.

Pizza

Who does not like some kind of pizza? We each have our personal preferences – some of us like pepperoni, some like sausage, others just want cheese. Others of us like a little bit of everything piled on. Pizza allows us so much variety and choice – it is a crowd favorite.

So, where and when did pizza become a dinner item? The first time the use of the actual word pizza was documented was in 997 A.D. in Gaeta, Italy. Pizza then spread across Italy, but was generally considered to be the food of the poor. Pizza or pizza pie has been on the Italian plate for over a century. But, surprisingly, it was not a popular dish there until after the second World War, when pizza became an absolute dining sensation in the U.S. The soldiers who had been stationed in Italy insisted that pizza be offered in the states and the real American pizza boom began.

Actually, pizza probably goes much further back in history. It was first made by the ancient Greeks who used the bread or crust as a replacement for a plate as they heaped their meats and vegetables on a bread slab.

In America, the pizza industry grosses well over $30 billion every year and about 1 out of every 5 restaurants are pizzerias. There are literally hundreds of pizza combinations available, from fruit to vegetable to meat, and often other ingredients are added. And most pizzerias deliver – bringing our pizza straight to our dining table.

One survey reported that over 93% of Americans order and eat pizza at least once every month. On Super Bowl Sunday, more than half of America orders pizza – making it the real pizza day of the year.

Mudslides

Very heavy rains in China triggered mudslides, washing away part of a town and killing 330 people. But heavy rains aren't the only things that can cause a mudslide. Mudslides are rivers of rock and earth that are saturated with water. Mudslides can be slow- or fast-moving and grow in both size and speed as they pick up trees, large stones, and anything else in their path downward.

Mudslides can occur at any time of the year and they strike without any warning, making them very dangerous. Mudslides occur in all 50 U.S. states and can happen with or without rainfall. Earthquakes, volcanic action, dramatic weather changes, and the steepening of mountain slopes by erosion increase the chances of a mudslide.

Wildfires also lead to mudslides because the burning kills the plants' roots that hold soil together. Because wildfires leave behind scorched slopes, California is especially prone to mudslides during and after major rainstorms. Overgrazing by livestock can also contribute to mudslides.

It is difficult to determine how likely a place is to have mudslides. They are known to occur in areas with a history of mudslides. The west coast of the U.S. is especially at risk of mudslides because of the earthquakes, rainfall, and wildfires that happen in that region.

Sand Castles

Let's talk seriously about sand castles. You probably think that sand castles are for toddlers and little kids with plastic buckets and shovels. Wrong! Did you know there are professional sand castle builders who create large, complicated, and beautiful sand creations for themselves, contests, and the public?

Like every creative profession, sand sculptors have their own construction techniques and unique vocabulary. Serious professional sand sculptors have three basic methods of compaction – that is, how the sand is kept together. The first and most intuitive method is what is called softpack. Softpack is simply patting moist sand into a mound that resembles the overall shape you are trying to create. The second method is called handstacking. This method adds pieces of one to the other and uses water and gravity to compact the sand, holding it in place as the piece is constructed. For huge sand art, which is growing in popularity, sand artists use prefabricated forms that give the sand shape, body, and durability. Serious sand sculptors use all three of these methods for varying parts of their sand art pieces.

Beach wedding getaways are now using sand sculptures as background décor for their big event. They have the artist sculpt a complex sand creation that has personal meaning for them and use it for backgrounds in the ceremony and photographs. Some of the creations are so difficult to make that sculptors must spend days putting them together.

Each year, there are serious contests judging sand castles and other intricate sculptures, with large cash awards given to the winners. Sand sculpture is a fulltime job for many adults who live near the coast where sand and sun are readily available for their craft.

The Joust

In movies and at Renaissance festivals held around the United States, men dressed in medieval-style armor joust with one another. Jousting is a sport where heavily armored men dressed as knights ride armored horses at full speed towards one another. The knights carry long pointed lances and try to land blows with their lance in an effort to unseat their opponent from his horse. It typically ends after a rather violent and loud clash when one knight's lance wins with a solid blow, or knocks their opponent off his steed.

In medieval times, jousting was a sport for nobles and knights, which allowed them to practice and hone skills they might later need on the battlefield. Jousting tournaments were actually extremely well planned and very formal. The nobles who wished to joust needed royal permission and the jousts were planned carefully months in advance. One common practice was to hire someone to joust for you, usually a jouster who would joust for anyone who paid the highest price. These jousters were called freelancers, a term we still use today.

Jousting's original aim was to kill your opponent, but in the 14th century the joust of peace was introduced. This new style awarded points for the quality of the strike and for shattering a lance. It is the style of jousting still used today.

Student Booklet

EXPOSITORY READING
PASSAGES

Urban Legends

An urban legend is actually a unique type of modern folk-lore. It usually consists of fictional tales that are presented as true events. The stories often have gruesome, humorous, or shocking elements. These legends are used to entertain others as well as for explanations (often tongue in cheek) for random odd objects, strange episodes, or bizarre animals.

Urban legends are spread easily in these days of social media. Some urban legends are very long lasting, and many have been retold over the years with only a few changes to suit regional cultures and modern tastes.

The most persistent urban legends could be plausible. One well known and often repeated example is that a mad killer is hiding in the back seat of a car one dark evening. He is about to spring and slay the driver, but another car following repeatedly shines bright headlights to alert the endangered driver. Another example was the recurring legend that the Procter & Gamble Company was in cahoots with devil worshippers. The company's nineteenth-century trademark had some odd markings that suggested to some people Satanic messages. The legend was believed by so many consumers that the company's business was negatively affected, and they discontinued the trademark.

Urban legends told often enough become considered truths. People who believe that the legends are real will strongly defend those legends. An example is the outrage of police officers when informed that poisoned Halloween treats given by strangers (causing periodic societal panics) occur extremely rarely, if at all.

Rabies

In the movie "Old Yeller," a tear-jerking moment occurs when the dog, named Old Yeller, must be shot by his young owner due to wild, angry, aggressive behavior and foaming at the mouth. Old Yeller had contracted rabies and the only solution to stop the spread of the disease and save the family was to destroy the animal.

Rabies is one of the most common zoonotic diseases on earth; that is, it is a virus passed from animals to humans. The overwhelming majority of rabies cases in animals reported in the United States each year occur in wild animals like raccoons, skunks, bats, and foxes. The rabies virus is a virus that is considered a global health threat. The virus is found on all continents except Antarctica.

The rabies virus is typically spread through the bite of a rabid infected mammal. Early symptoms can include fever and tingling at the site of exposure. Later symptoms include fever, headache, excess salivation – the foaming of the mouth, muscle spasms, paralysis, and mental confusion. In humans, the rabies virus causes an overwhelming inflammation of the brain virtually untreatable with current day antibiotics. There is no specific treatment for rabies and once symptoms appear, the disease is nearly always fatal.

The rabies virus kills over 55,000 people in the world each year and the majority of these deaths, 99%, are due to rabid dog bites. Most deaths are in Asia and Africa with 40% of the victims children under the age of 15. In the Americas, bats are now the major source of human rabies deaths. Rabies is generally considered to be a neglected tropical disease in that it predominantly affects vulnerable impoverished people. Although effective human vaccines exist for rabies, they are simply not readily available to populations who live in remote rural locales.

Elimination of rabies deaths is possible through vaccination of dogs and prevention of dog bites in most of the world. There are two treatment protocols for the rabies virus for humans. There is a rabies vaccine for pre-exposure immunization usually given to people who might be exposed to rabid animals in their work or travels. And there is a post-exposure vaccine first developed by Louis Pasteur and colleagues in 1885 that can save lives when initiated promptly after the bite. More than 15 million people worldwide receive a post-bite vaccination preventing hundreds of thousands of rabies deaths annually.

Hoarding

Hoarding and caching are behaviors observed in many bird species and in rodents. Most animal caches or hoards are of food. The animal is prepping for cold or inclement weather during which food availability may be limited. Some human beings also accumulate food or other items and have significant difficulty discarding or parting with possessions, regardless of the actual value of the objects.

Periods of civil unrest or threat of imminent natural disaster may lead people to hoard food, water, gasoline, munitions, and other essentials that they believe will soon be in short supply. Survivalists often stockpile large supplies of items in anticipation of a large-scale disaster event or apocalypse.

Hoarders are people who are anxious or experience extreme discomfort about discarding unneeded items or items that lack any value due to a feeling of attachment to these items. Compulsive hoarders will associate certain, typically commonplace, objects to their own sense of self, or even attribute certain human characteristics to inanimate objects. They can place extraordinary value or importance to objects that others rightly consider trash. These people can suffer intense distress at the thought of disposing of these belongings. Hoarding behaviors range from mild to severe.

Problems with hoarding gradually develop and are usually difficult to discern as the hoarder is usually quite secretive. Others, even those close to the individual, may not discover the extent of the hoarding until it has reached unsightly or unhealthy levels. In severe cases, the living quarters of such people are fire or health hazards.

There is no approved effective medical treatment specific to hoarding behavior. Additionally, people with hoarding disorder may not consider it a problem, making any treatment options challenging. At this time, the primary treatment for people with hoarding disorder is usually cognitive behavior therapy, which has had some success in curbing the behaviors.

STUDENT BOOKLET

EXPOSITORY READING PASSAGES

The Art of Mime

It is rare that people today see a mime performance – that is a person who is performing the art of mime. A mime or mime artist (from Greek mimos, "imitator, actor") is a person who uses mime as a performance art or theatrical form. Miming involves acting out a story through exaggerated body motions, without talking. It is usually a solo act with few props and simple sets.

Miming is an ancient performance art originating in ancient Rome and Greece. It was also very popular in Italy before the form reached France. Most believe the first mime performance was in the Theatre of Dionysus in Athens. Actors wore masks and performed outdoors, before audiences of 10,000 or more, at festivals to honor the God of theatre, Dionysus.

In the early 1800s, Parisian mime Jean-Gaspard Deburau created some performance standards that influenced the modern mimes, including totally silent performances and white, painted faces so as to make the performers facial expressions more obvious. Others developed what is labeled corporeal mime, a type of pantomime using the human body contortions and movements to express emotion.

The most famous mime of the last century is certainly Marcel Marceau who created the stage persona Bip the Clown. Marceau was the first modern mime celebrity who considered mime the "art of silence". He performed professionally worldwide to wildly enthusiastic audiences for over 60 years.

The American Mime Theatre is a professional performing company and training school based in New York City. Founded in 1952, it is the oldest continuing professional mime company in the United States. Mime in America is a blend of many styles. Mime has long been considered to be a European import, but American mime is somewhat of a melting pot, with much experimentation straying from classic mime in many ways.

The Four Fundamental Forces of Nature

Physicists have identified and can mathematically calculate what they consider the four fundamental forces of nature. These four are the gravitational and electromagnetic forces, which produce significant long-range effects and whose properties can be seen directly in everyday life, and the strong and weak subatomic forces, which produce effects at a minuscule, subatomic distance and regulate nuclear interactions.

Gravitational force, surprisingly, is generally considered to be a weak force. It is, however, very long-ranged and acts between any two pieces of matter anywhere in the universe, as mass itself is the source of this force.

The electromagnetic force causes both electric and magnetic effects, such as the repulsion between similar electrical charges or the interaction of magnetic fields. It is long-ranged, but much weaker than the strong subatomic force. This force can both attract or repel, but acts only between pieces of matter carrying electrical charge. Electricity, magnetism, and light are all products of this force.

The weak subatomic force is responsible for radioactive decay and interactions between neutrinos. Neutrinos are leptons, elementary particles very similar to electrons, but without an electrical charge. The weak subatomic force has a very short range and, as the label indicates, it is very weak. The weak force is the cause of Beta decay, the conversion of a neutron into a proton, an electron, and an antineutrino.

The strong subatomic force actually causes interactions and is very powerful, but very short-ranged. This force literally holds the nuclei of atoms together and is conveyed by particles called gluons, often labeled the messenger particle. Quarks interact by emitting and absorbing gluons, literally exchanging gluons. Thus, the quarks inside of the protons and neutrons are kept together by the exchange of the strong subatomic force.

There are scientists who posit that when the universe was very young and the temperatures very high, all four forces were one singularity. They speculate that as the temperature dropped, gravitation was the first to separate, followed by the other 3 forces. And for a period in the life of the universe, the weak, electromagnetic, and strong forces were combined into one single force. When the temperature dropped further, these forces separated from each other, with the strong force separating first followed by the electromagnetic and weak forces. This process by which these forces separated is labeled spontaneous symmetry breaking, a phenomenon in which small fluctuations, in this case temperature change, cross a critical point and decide the system's fate.

Mitochondrian

The mitochondrion (plural mitochondria) is a double-membrane-bound organelle found in most eukaryotic organisms. Eukaryotic organisms, such as human beings, consist of cells with DNA in the form of chromosomes contained within a defined nucleus. A mitochondrion contains outer and inner membranes composed of phospholipid bilayers and proteins. Because of this double-membraned organization, there are five distinct compartments within the mitochondrion. There is the outer mitochondrial membrane, the intermembrane space (the space between the outer and inner membranes), the inner mitochondrial membrane, the cristae space (formed by infoldings of the inner membrane), and the matrix (space within the inner membrane).

The outer membrane covers the organelle and encases it, much like a skin. The inner membrane folds over many times and creates layered structures called cristae. The fluid contained in the mitochondria is called the matrix.

The multiple infoldings of the inner membrane increases the surface area inside the organelle. Since many of the chemical reactions happen on the inner membrane, the increased surface area creates more opportunities for reactions to occur.

Mitochondria are unique organelles because they have their own ribosomes and DNA present in the matrix. There are also structures called granules that may control concentrations of ions. Scientists are still exploring the role and activity of granules.

Often called the powerhouse organelle, the mitochondria supply cellular energy by generating adenosine triphosphate (ATP), a source of energy for the cells. This process is labeled cellular respiration. Mitochondria are critical in other tasks, such as cellular differentiation, cellular signaling, cell growth, and cell death. In humans, the number of mitochondria varies by cell type, being most abundant in liver cells with about 1000 to 2000 mitochondria per cell. They are especially abundant in cells and parts of cells that are associated with active processes, such as the liver, and average about 50–100 per cell in the body. Cells have the ability to produce more mitochondria as needed for additional cellular respiration, and can combine mitochondria to make larger ones.

STUDENT BOOKLET
EXPOSITORY READING PASSAGES

Spring Term (I)
GRADES 10 – 12

Where Do Clothes Go?

You probably live in a community where there is a drop off station or other resource at a church or charity for discarding used clothing and household items. Donating used items is a way of throwing away clothing or other objects without actually throwing them away. We believe we are actually doing the world a service by giving our used or out of fashion clothing to those less fortunate. Almost 5 billion pounds of clothing are donated by Americans each year, but surprisingly only about 10 percent of the clothing donated is resold in the retail stores of most charities.

The other 90%? The charity shop sells the garments by weight to professional textile recyclers. Employees at the recycling plant work at a breakneck pace to sort the garments judging wearability and analyzing quality and fiber. This sorting process determines the next destination of the donated clothing. It can end up in landfills, be recycled into insulation or other materials, or be sold in the markets of Sub-Saharan Africa.

The clothing that can be worn again is shipped by the tons to African countries in one hundred-pound bales. African buyers in these countries purchase these directly from the recycler with one caveat - the bales are not allowed to be opened or inspected by the buyer until the purchase is completed. The quality of the purchased clothing is dependent on the sorting method used by the recycler and, unfortunately, there have been many documented instances when the African purchaser has opened merchandise that is virtually unwearable.

Recently, many African nations have attempted to ban and/or restrict these clothing imports and practices. These countries have done so to boost the native textiles industries in their own nations and to maintain the traditional cultural dress.

On Broadway

Broadway theater, known to most as "Broadway," refers to the theatrical performances played in the 41 professional theaters located in the Theater District and Lincoln Center along Broadway, in Midtown Manhattan, New York City. This famous street in Manhattan has become one of the worldwide leaders in stage entertainment, along with London's West End theater, and is considered to represent the highest level of commercial theater in the English-speaking world.

The origins of Broadway history in New York began in 1750 when Thomas Kean and Walter Murray opened their theater company on Nassau Street. This theater seated 280 patrons and typically put on Shakespearian plays and ballad operas. Theater performances ceased in the city during the Revolutionary War, but resumed in 1798. The popularity of theater led to the building of another much larger venue, The Park Theater, with seating for 2000.

The Park Theater was a very popular and well-attended city attraction. Accordingly, many other theaters, such as the famous Bowery Theatre, were built. Blackface minstrel shows began to be performed and rivalled the theatrical production works of Shakespeare in popularity. One of the premier nightspots in New York was Niblo's Garden, which produced both musical and non-musical acts.

In 1849 the Astor Place Theatre opened and caused, for the first time, a sense among New Yorkers that different socioeconomic classes of people did not share entertainment interest. A riot ensued when the lower-class audience that frequented the Bowery took umbrage to the perceived snobbery of the upper-class audiences that attended the Astor. As a result, this riot separated theater audiences into differing social strata as the upper classes attended the opera, the middle class attended melodramas and minstrel shows, while the working class attended the variety shows.

Today the theaters of Broadway attract over 10 million attendees each year. The works performed there have vastly enriched the arts throughout the world, providing laughter, drama, music, and dance.

The Origin of Dogs

The domestic dog, Canis familiaris, is a member of the genus Canis (canines), which forms part of the wolf-like canids, and is the most common terrestrial carnivore on earth. It was long posited that domestic dogs were direct descendants of the gray wolf.

In 1999, a study emphasized that, while molecular genetic data seem to support the origin of dogs from wolves, dogs may have descended from a now extinct species of canid whose closest living relative was the wolf. The dog's lineage may have been contributed to from a ghost population. Further research has demonstrated that the dog and the gray wolf are taxonomically related, but modern wolves are not closely related to the wolves that were first domesticated, implying that the direct ancestor of the dog is extinct.

What we call dogs were just a type of wolf when our ancestors tamed and began to manage them. There are two conflicting theories about when and where dogs were domesticated.

One theory holds that humans domesticated dogs for the first time in Europe more than 15,000 years ago. Opposing researchers believe the domestication happened approximately 12,500 years ago in Central Asia or China. The Paleolithic Age dogs are the first researchers can identify as having human contact through anthropological findings. These dogs were directly associated with human hunting camps in Europe over 30,000 years ago. Dogs at that time most closely resembled the current

Siberian Husky, but were larger in size, more like today's large herding dogs.

The dog was the first species to be domesticated and has been selectively bred over the centuries for various behaviors, tasks, sensory capabilities, and physical traits and attributes. Humans fed them, bred them, and spread them from continent to continent. While other wolf descendants died out, dogs grew into a new species. In many aspects, human beings actually invented the dog.